MW01180694

MOVE

A Simple Understanding to Achieving

By Freeman

Cover Illustration By A.Gause

Move: A Simple Understanding to Achieving

copyright©2014 E.G. Freeman

MOVE

A SIMPLE UNDERSTANDING TO ACHIEVING

E.G.FREEMAN

Illustration by A.Gause

3/2014

ISBN-13: 9781499187038
ISBN-10: 1499187033

NOTE: There is a space at the back of this book for you to take notes if you choose.

Thanks

I thank the Lord God for His Blessings and Mercies in my life that He saw in me the Little Sparrow and gave me something to say.

Forward

I would like to dedicate this book to the young people, mentors, social workers, pastors and ministers, gangs members, those on drugs, and those who cannot seem to find the inspiration to get themselves to the next level. I wasn't sure how I was going to write this book, but I knew something needed to be said. I learned certain things about life and the realities and illusions that can cause anyone to lose sight of their greatness, and how simple things we never pay attention to can boost us forward in life.

For the longest time, I used to wish someone would just give me a chance to prove myself. I would think things like, "If only I could get a job over there", or "If only I could show them how this would work better for them". I wanted other people who I felt were accomplished to possibly give me a chance at anything, and then my life would be better. The problem with this type of thinking is that all of my determination was being put into someone else's dream and idea of success and no one cared about my dreams. I didn't realize that God had a plan for me. I was always disappointed because I put numerous hours of hard work to make someone else happy, instead I needed to make myself happy. I just didn't know how.

I decided in 2012 that I was going to live a better life and I was going to change the direction in which my life was going. Believe me, I wasn't really going anywhere. I had some bad relationships and didn't care about much, except for my children. I was only really living for them. My life had become habitually boring and full of excuses of why I could not do anything further with myself. I was stuck.

I knew that I wanted better for myself, but I was not giving myself the permission or the chance to get up, change my mind, and just move in a different direction. I needed to take charge and speak a new existence into my life. So one day I just knelt down and prayed and got really serious with God, and I laid my life down and asked Him to be in a part of everything I do. I needed God to know that I know that I am nothing without Him in my life. I was starting to redefine myself, and as I opened my mind to understanding, I began to see more and learn more.

The purpose of this book is to inspire those of you who have goals and dreams, but have somehow stopped working on them--to continue your path and remember your goals. I want you to remember your faith and the abilities that God gave you. During my self-development efforts and trying to refine who I am, I realized the things I am interested in and realized what I wanted to be committed to in my life. I always had dreams of doing something and I always felt like I could do anything. However, my heart could never commit to doing any one thing. I always felt like I am going to miss out on something, but did not realize that everything I needed was already in me. I always believed that I was good at everything I did and still do, but nothing ever made me feel whole heartedly committed, until now. So I want to share with you what is not easy to do—ACHIEVE and be HAPPY while doing it. As you read this book you will find yourself wanting to be a leader, a better mother or father, a better student or in general being a better person, an Achiever.

I also intend on giving those of you who have goals and dreams, an understanding on how to achieve them without feeling as though you have compromised your life and values. This is important: I want to share with you, the reader, about how God can make things happen in your life almost immediately. Remind yourself of this daily and pray for it.

> *Blessed is the one who does not walk in step with the wicked or stand in the way that sinners take or sit in the company of mockers,*
> [2] *but whose delight is in the law of the LORD, and who meditates on his law day and night.*
> [3] *That person is like a tree planted by streams of water, which yields its fruit in season*
> *and whose leaf does not wither--whatever they do prosper.*
>
> *Psalms 1:1-3*

While you are reading this book, you will start to feel your mind changing and your chemical make-up begin to evolve you. By time you are finished reading this book, your life will change and you will be transformed into someone who is committed to achieving your goals and living a committed life for yourself, and so I say, "Get up and MOVE". This book is just a short look at how I learned how to MOVE.

<u>CONTENTS</u>

Move: A Simple Understanding to Achieving

Chapter 1:

What Do You Live For Right Now?

A life mentor once taught me that you have to be committed to yourself and your dreams in order for your body to obey and move you forward. She said that you cannot be just interested in it; you have to be committed to it. Well, what is the difference? The difference is that to be interested in something, you will only do what is comfortable to do. You will do what everybody else does. You will do what is the easiest thing to do. To be committed, you will do what is absolutely necessary to achieve your goal. You will do what is not easy to do. You will learn everything you need to learn, change everything you need to change, and whatever it is that you need to do you will do it to achieve your goal. So many people think that they are committed to themselves and their goals, yet there is no hard work put forth to prove it and get there. The second any obstacle comes their way or when someone has the audacity to say something in opposition to their goal, they say that they can't do it.

So, I ask what level of control you have on your life right now because this is the question that starts you to looking into yourself, and getting you to think about what you are currently doing with yourself. Some of you may say that you are living in the present, but moving forward. If this is so, then what do you worry about? Maybe your finances, maybe your family member, maybe your job, your bills, your current situation. If this is the case, then you are worrying about the things in your life that are naturally taken care of for you when your mind and lifestyle are in sync and MOVING FORWARD to greatness.

When I ask, where is your life now? I am asking you to think about your life experiences and bring your experience from the past to the present, whether positive or negative. You have to see that every experience in your life IS what was necessary to get you to this point in your life. Stop making excuses about the things that have happened to you. Stop bringing them forward and feeling sorry for yourself; as though you need permission from the experiences to be happy and move forward. No matter how negative the circumstance was, it made you who you are today, mentally. Now it is up to you to take that situation and USE it to lift yourself to greater. You have to heal from the negative circumstances and allow yourself the permission to use your own experiences to create better experiences as well as be a better person.

When I was self-absorbed, I was overly sensitive. Everything offended me. I enjoyed feeling as though I was entitled to others emotions. Emotions are a temporary distraction. At some point you have to continue your motion forward. I had to ask myself these questions. What are you doing with your life right now, and where is your life destined to be? Why haven't you achieved the greater goals in your life?

Stop reading and get a pad of paper and write down, in list form, the things you have gone through in your life. Whether you think it was positive or negative, and be specific. —write them down. By the way, make sure it is a pad of paper or notebook that only you write in.

Example

_ *We went on family vacations every year to____.*

_ *My mom used to teach me how to make bread.*

_ *I used to write in a journal vs. I have always write in a journal.*

_ *I used to get in fights at school with boys all the time.*

_ *I started having sex at 13.*

_ *My uncle/aunt used to feel on me.*

_ *I learned how to change a tire at 13.*

_ *I was raped.*

_ *I was always at the top of my class in school*

_ *I took a life skills class when I was 16.*

_ *I hated _____ school.*

_ *I gave my life to the Lord and was baptized.*

_ *We used to wear uniforms in high school.*

_ *My ex-husband left me for another woman.*

_ *My boyfriend after my husband was a cheater.*

_ *I joined the military or I went to college and got _____ certification/degree.*

_ *In 19__ I had my first child.*

It may seem a little insignificant, but it is not. The purpose of writing this down is for evaluation purposes. Use as much paper as you need. When you are finished, place a number in front of each experience putting them in order to how they happened in your life, if you can remember. On the right side of the experience place a checkmark next to the experiences you think were negative.

Take your time. When you have completed this, write down, on another list, what you think you have learned from each negative situation. Take your time. This IS your life. Once you have done this, and then take a look at those things you have learned and recognize how you make your decisions today based on what you have experienced.

The average person will take the experiences they live and use the momentary lessons learned to set boundaries and standards in their life. These boundaries have caused you to not climb the mountains in your life. When your guard is up you block yourself from experiences and growth. You have to allow yourself to use your past experiences to maneuver and move around, getting fear out of the way. Understand that you have to climb these hills and mountains *(your difficulties)*, face the people that you are avoiding, make yourself think differently, and do the things that are difficult to do. To be greater and do greater you have to get through the smaller difficulties first. Otherwise, you repeat yourself until you have mastered it. Have you ever asked yourself, "Why do I keep going through this?" Well, think about it. You haven't made the right decisions or changes in your life to ensure that you are not repeating your history over and over again. Don't try to just do enough to impress other people, making it look like you're doing something different, but in the background you're doing and thinking something else. YOU HAVE TO do what it takes to make a complete change. When you are dissatisfied enough with yourself or circumstances (100%) your body will produce the Will to make a change. Now you have to decide for yourself that the change is necessary and that you are committed to making the change. 100% dissatisfaction creates 100% change.

Stop telling yourself that you can't do something because it reminds you of the past. So what if it reminds you of the past, now what? Take the memory of the past experience and use it to get around the obstacles that you already know are there. You have an advantage and these are your maneuvering tools! When you give these tools more value than what they are, then you are giving yourself permission to live lower than who you are. This is why you have only gone so far in your life, and then you settle for the next best thing that seems easier to do, or you settle for whatever is given to you along the way. If you have goals or dreams that you want to accomplish and can't seem to get there, you have to evaluate your system of belief and achieving. You have to change how you think. Life experiences are meant to make you wiser, but not to stop you from moving forward.

If you are only interested in achieving your goals you are making excuses for why those things that you consider to be negative are good enough reasons to stop what you are doing. If you are committed to your goals you will stop making excuses and blaming others or your circumstances. Stop blaming your circumstances and situations for why you are not doing better or greater in your life. Your situation, education level, physical capability, your finances, or any other reason you may have, deserves no attention for how you are to achieve your goals. Make your mental note and put your focus on how you CAN and WILL achieve your goals.

Look at your list of life experiences and notice the lessons learned. Now think about how these lessons have helped you to reach the goals that you have accomplished so far to this point. Think about your conscious efforts you have taken to direct yourself to get over certain obstacles. It was the tools you were given and learned along the way, from your experiences that allowed you to get to this point. Those experiences were necessary to reach this point in your life. A mistake that most of you make is that you take the experiences from your past, fear of failure, finances, and any other reason you can give and partially shut down your goals or dreams. This is as far as you go, and you never achieve much higher than where you are today. When you do this it stunts your process of achieving. You are allowing thoughts of fear, denial, disagreement, disapproval, opposition, and rejection to take over your mind and form a chemical reaction in your brain that poisons your affirmatives to achieve because it is easier to just sit down. I call this the "Underdeveloped Mind". Others call it the "Poverty Mindset". The reason I call it as such is because you have not allowed your mind to experience its greatness. You stopped your mental development to overcoming difficulties and now you have allowed obstacles that have nothing to do with your achievement to stop you. The thing about an obstacle is that it is not of itself infinite—it is, only if you see it that way. There is always a way around it. For example; if there is a log in your path, it is not infinitely long or wide. You can walk around it, walk or climb over it, or chop it in half and move it out of your way. Don't make obstacles bigger than you.

Maybe you have allowed other people's experiences to stop you and/or make you feel like you cannot do something. No matter what, when you have an underdeveloped mind, you watch others achieve while you stand by believing that you will never have your chance because no one will give you a chance. Deceptive intelligence becomes your friend and you stop achieving.

When going through difficult times, prayer always helps. By the way, you should always be looking at your motives and why you want to do what you want to do.

What do you want to do? Why do you want to do it? The Creator has created you to be successful in all that you do. Therefore being a good person to yourself first and then to others is important. Rely on the power from within, and read your goals that you have written down every day. Read and understand your goals in order to get through your moments of deceptive intelligence and dysfunctional breakdowns, which rationalizes why you should not do what you are committing yourself to. Understand that the dreams God gave you are yours, and specific for you. You own it; it is only when you do nothing with it that God takes it away and gives it to someone else. Have you ever had an idea come to mind and you ponder on it for a long time? You never write it down, and eventually you start believing it is nothing so you do nothing with it? What happens? Next thing you know, you will see or hear of someone who is doing it, and you try to convince yourself that you thought of it first or a long time ago. Well, you did nothing with it, so now you have nothing to do with it. Write your goals & dreams down and remind yourself of them every day. Learn to respect & love what God has put in you. When you nurture, develop, respect and work hard for self, you are showing and proving your love for yourself and for The Creator. I learned that Love is the greatest creative force in the universe. If it is the GREATEST creative force then shouldn't people want to master LOVE, especially loving yourself? You need this in order to maintain goals. You need to love what is inside of you.

So if your goal is to be healthy and live a healthy life spiritually, mentally and physically then you should be doing things that contribute to good spiritual, mental and physical health. In order to maintain this you have to continue to feed yourself LIFE mentally and physically. To talk yourself into why it would be alright to drink beer every day, or eat fried foods every day is sabotage to yourself and when you feel sick you say "Oh it was gonna happen anyway". Good health does not happen on its own. At a certain point in your life your body begins to get old if it is not given the necessary things to be alive and renew. It takes your special efforts and conscious decisions to happen. Doing the things that are difficult to do that you know are good, and have good end results are the things that you have to hold on to. We will talk more on this later when we discuss how to make your changes.

Most people work really hard at setting goals, but when it comes to achieving the goals, they do the easiest thing possible to get themselves a "little piece of the pie" *(games of chance)*. How big is your goal? Do you think that you have large goals? If you say, "Yes my goals or dreams are large" then I ask you this. When you achieve that goal then what will you do? Your goals and dreams are never too big. They can never be big enough. I say that to say this; some goals may take a lifetime to achieve, and some are the ones you achieve along the way. Just because you have achieved one goal does not mean that you're done. Always keep in your mind that your life is fulfilled by moving forward.

Chapter 2:

God's Desire for You

When you want something, what is the first thing you do? Well, if it is something that is easily attainable your Will picks you up with no effort and you move towards that which you want and you go and get it. It's easy as 1, 2, 3, right? What happens if what you want takes more effort or it seems more far reaching? It does not seem like you can just get up and go and get it. It does not seem as easy as getting up in the morning and getting ready for work. Immediately your mind starts to think of all the things that are necessary to attain such a thing.

There is no such fact as; you do not know how to get it. You knew how to get what you want since you were a child. From children to the drug addict on the street, all knows how to achieve a goal. It's already in you. You have to be committed to it. A baby naturally finds a way to achieve its goals because he or she has no choice but to evolve, so they watch and learn. They try one tactic and if it is not successful, then he or she will try something else. Failure is not an option, even if he or she has to cry out to you to pick him or her up to get it. To a baby, that is success. No matter how negative or positive the means to get there is, they are achieving their goal. How is it that you allow a baby to be more successful at achieving a goal than you? Now I am not condoning negative behavior to achieve a goal. Babies don't know any better, you do. Babies not too long ago came from the Creator. They are closer in time to the experience of God and obeying His will than you and I are. You will understand this as I explain throughout this chapter.

What if I told you that you were made for GREATNESS? What if I told you that your goals are not big enough? What if I told you that God has a bigger plan for you? When God wants something

He speaks it into existence. God says, "Let there Be…" and it Is. You are the only being that is both made and created by God. You were a made Being in the likeness of God. Let me explain. According to, Merriam-Webster Dictionary, the word, **Created** means; to bring into existence, not evolved from something else. The word, **Made** means; to prepare from several ingredients, coming from another source. In other words Created is to form something from nothing, and Made is to form something from something else. You are the only being that God made in His image (like Him), but yet created you from His mind.

In the book of Genesis God spoke to bring His creation into existence, and He also spoke *to* His creation for it to bring forth others. Look at the Book of *Genesis 1:1—"In the beginning God created the Heavens and the Earth…"* *Genesis 1:3—"Then God said, 'Let there be light'; and there was Light"*. In the first part of Genesis God is Creating, but then He starts speaking to His creation and commanding His creation to produce (make) more for Him. Why would God do this? God is the Creator of the Heavens and the Earth.

Why would He want His creation to imitate Him? God needed His creation to be in obedience to His Will. He gave the Creation instructions of what He wants. *Genesis 1:20—"Then God said, 'Let the waters <u>abound with</u> an abundance of living creatures…and God blessed them saying be fruitful and multiply…"* *Genesis 1:24—"Then God said, 'Let the <u>earth bring forth</u> the living creature according to its kind…"* Now God did not say for the earth to bring forth the living creatures according to Me because the earth cannot make His kind.

Only God could have created and made Himself so He did, in His image and of His likeness. So, in

Genesis 1:26—"Then God said, 'Let Us make man in Our image, according to Our likeness; let him have dominion...Then God blessed them: and said unto them, Be fruitful , and multiply... " What is the "Us" and the "Our". It is later revealed in the Bible to be, God the Father, God the Son, and God the Holy Spirit. God made man of Himself and gave man instructions to rule the earth and all in it.

God made you from Him; therefore you are sustained by God. You cannot be a nonproductive being. You have to be that being that God wants you to be. You cannot live on the things in life that are unhealthy or adds no life giving essentials. You cannot live without his words. He is your life vein. You are born connected to Him. If you are pulled away or you pull yourself away from Him then you die. You may not physically die immediately, but you start to participate in thoughts and activities that will kill you spiritually, kill your mental strength, and eventually physically. Your spiritual connection is the most important because that is where God speaks to you, in your spirit. Your obedience to God happens first in your spirit.

When that is gone, not too far after your physical starts to wither away too. *Ephesians 2:1—"And you did He make alive, when you were dead through your trespasses and sins…". John 10:10— "…I came that they may have life, and may have it abundantly."* Throughout the Bible it speaks of how God created you to have life and be alive. Why not live that way?

Are you starting to understand that you are God's desire? God wanted and made you to be just like Him. God had a desire for a companion and He made the companion in His likeness. But just like God had a desire, man had one too and God knew exactly what man needed because He too desired out of His loneliness, so He made woman as a companion for man. This is love. Love makes and creates for its companion.

God created you with a Will, therefore you have the ability to make a choice. Only a creation with a Will can love. Why would God give you the ability to love? God made you so that you can love Him. He loves you so much that He wants you to be able to love. He wants you to experience love. He wants you to show your love to Him and profess your love to Him. When you express your love to Him, He will express His Love back to you. God is a giving God, and He does not receive without giving back.

Are you seeing where I am going with this? Now, how does this connect with you and your goals or dreams? You must have goals, dreams, or desires. As a human being, your aspirations should be right in line with God's word because God is the One who gave those goals, dreams, and desires to you.

Therefore, when your greatest desire is to want God in everything you do and express your love for Him, He will bless all that you do and make your aspirations work for His glory allowing you to do great works.

God's gifts are blessings. When He gives you a blessing it is for you. You must grasp that blessing and learn how to use it. You have to understand that it is not some hand-me-down. You have to nurture that gift and take care of it. When you buy a new outfit or new shoes nobody can tell you anything. You make sure it is hung up on a hanger in the closet, and nicely ironed when you are ready to wear it. You make sure your shoes don't have any scuffs or marks on them because you want to show your outfit like this is how you are all the time. The same goes for God's blessings or gifts to you. You must take it with honor and nurture it. Work hard to maintain it. Make it as if it has been a part of your life all the time. It is when you feel like it's nothing or not important that you will not work for it or work hard to keep up with it. You may lose it.

To sabotage your own blessing is defeating yourself. Most people that do not achieve anything, let alone their goals do not achieve because of unknowing self-sabotage. If you never take ownership of your blessing or gift, you will never achieve the greatness that God has for you. That goes for all blessings that you have. Take care of all of your blessing. When you face your goal with the same enthusiasm as when you started, regardless of the losses, downfalls, frustrations, and nonsuccesses (which will be there), your commitment and faith will grow stronger and make you stronger. I asked once before, are you interested in achieving your goal or committed to achieving your goal?

The more you realize this and move out on faith, the more your faith will grow and the greater your work becomes. By the way, when God gives you a dream, He will usually give you a gift or talent to accommodate it. You have to make up in your mind that you want God to be involved in your life.

Chapter 3:

Committing the Realest Love There Is

What do you love? What is important to you? Are you important to you? It is a known fact that Love is the greatest creative force in the universe. Make the decision to love yourself first. After all that I have said so far you have no choice but to love yourself. If God loves you and created and made you so that He can love you, then why wouldn't you love you? The decisions you make in your life have to be that of better and greater consequence. Don't become what you have been through. Respect and learn what you have been through so that you can understand your path. You cannot say that you love you and not love God. You cannot say you love yourself and everyone sees you doing OTHER THAN that which expresses your love for yourself and God. Every decision and every action you take is an expression of your true self and what you know you are worthy of.

So many people live their lives saying that they love themselves, but are dishonest, careless, disrespectful, hateful towards others, and non-spiritual. When you love yourself, everything you do will reflect that you do. It is only when you love yourself that you can love others. You won't have to say it out loud to others. They will see it in your actions. How can you love someone else and not love yourself, except that you have devalued yourself. You were not made to be of service to another except through your own love for yourself to another. Otherwise you are a slave to that which you claim to love.

No one person is perfect. You have imperfections and may have dysfunctional behaviors, but who are you? Based on the previous chapter, you should have a good idea of who you are. Now that you have examined the root of who you are and why you were created, it's up to you to decide how much you love yourself. Open up to yourself and see the truth. Accept those imperfections about yourself and realize what needs to change to make your forward step. If you cannot accept yourself and love yourself enough to make any life changing decisions then you will continue to travel the same cycle. Be honest with yourself and look at what is hard to see, and realize that you have a decision to make to change your mind, to see it differently and love who you are.

It is only when you love yourself enough that you can see the changes that are needed, and you are able to make the decision to change your mind. In this instance only love can create a new person in you and start to make a chemical change in your brain. The chemical change begins your "Aha" moment. When you start to love the person you are and can make the decision to change your mind to change, you start to attract the things to yourself that are needed to make the change. You also start to clean house and remove the things from your life that are excuses and not a part of who you can now see yourself becoming. You are beginning to be responsible for yourself and your actions. You are becoming your true self.

This is not the end of it. Do not make the mistake of taking this much and not continue to read. I told you in an earlier chapter that God gave you a will (ability to make a decision and make it happen). Because of your will you have the ability to love. Yes, God can help you through your tough times and tough decisions, but He has already helped you by giving you the will. Now it is up to you to make the proper decisions for your life and get yourself through. Think about your actions. Remember, if you love yourself, it will reflect upon your actions and the things you do. I love myself; therefore I am a decision maker that proves that I am alive and true to myself and God. Can you say this? Are you making the decisions to be true to yourself and love yourself?

Your life is the reality YOU create. If you want to be a happy person, then make the decision to be a happy person. It is your choice and it is not dependent upon your circumstance or your situation. What is important to you? If your life is full of problems, it is because those problems are what you are making important to you. Change your mind. There is no greater love then the love that God has put in you to love yourself.

Chapter 4:

Realizing Your Goals or Dreams

When I was a child, I was very capable of almost everything I tried to do. I was very talented and had many skills. This carried on through adulthood and made a confidence in me that made me realize that anything is possible. I used to tell people that I was kind of a jack-of-all-trades, but I never committed to any *one* thing. I never took steps to accomplish a goal or dream, until I joined the military. The military will give you your goal and make you accomplish the goal. After that reality check, I started doing things at a higher level of thinking. I started talking to myself when something became difficult. I would talk myself into making it happen and being successful.

As I got older, my goals became greater and because other things (circumstances and situations) were more important to me, I allowed those things to become excuses for me. My goals started to seem to be impossible to reach because I did not understand that those things were not part of who I am, nor were I to become them. It wasn't until the moment when I realized that I had been sabotaging myself and my achievements, and changed my mind that things started to turn around for me. I needed to put my efforts into what was important for my life and what God had designed for me. When I made the move towards loving myself and what God has designed for me, the impossible started to become possible. What I felt to be important in my life changed how I accomplished my goals. I fell in love with myself and who I really am.

I said all that to say this. Your goals may change, or they may stay the same. Some people have goals from when they were a child, and some people may have goals that only just recently popped up. It does not matter. What matters is—there's a natural skill or gift that you have that helps you to be successful in your process? Or, do you need education to help you achieve your skill?

What are your natural talents and skills? Do you have any? Do you like these things that you can do naturally? It always helps if you can do something naturally within the line of your goals or dreams. Earlier I talked about how God can give you a dream (goal, idea), and when He does He will usually give you a gift or talent to accommodate that dream or goal. God has a purpose for you, therefore He is going to give you something that is for you to use, and not for others to tell you when to use it or if you can use it at all. It is from God, so use it.

Your goals are an important aspect of achieving. You have to have something or somewhere to reach. You have to write them down and be exact, be specific to achieve it. Knowing your goal and seeing your goal written down will help you to stay on track towards that goal. Everything you have ever seen and heard in your life time was someone else's dream and goal. They thought about it and worked hard to bring it into existence. You have to do the same. Never think that your goals are stupid or insignificant. Just remember the love you have for yourself to achieve your goals. Just because no one has ever heard about it before does not mean it is impossible or stupid.

Everything in front of you right now was someone else's dream. You may ask yourself, how do I set a goal to advance myself from here to there? Or, how do I move forward? Well, the first things you need to do are realize where "**there**" is, and then have a goal or idea. Where do you want (not hope) to be, what do you want (not hope) to accomplish, who do you want to be, what kind of person do you want to be? Is there a gift?

Write all of this down. When you decide what kind of person you want to be and who you are going to be, write it down as your top priority. Create your Vision. We will talk about this in the next chapter. When you write your goal down, you are writing what you are visualizing for yourself.

I want you to take a moment and sit back and think about your life right now. What can you do better? What are your needs? What are the things that you want? Why do you want or need these things? Look around yourself at everything. Every single thing that you are wearing, doing, looking at was thought up by someone else. That person followed their rightful path and did something useful.

Now that you understand that you are on the path to greatness, you need to analyze and evaluate your goals. Keep your mind on this path; continue to think about your rise to higher levels. Continue to empower yourself and know that with God's help nothing is impossible. Understand that God has given you a new mind so don't fill it with all of your old thoughts. He has given you the ability to change your mind and your thoughts. Remember what I said earlier, your goals are never too big. Think about them and make your goals specific.

Be specific about what you want. The reason I say to be specific is because every desire has specific needs. If you want to be the best cook in the world you are going to have specific needs. You will need to learn about the kitchen, utensils, cooking, chemistry, people's likes and dislike and so much more. You will think about all the ways you can making your cooking the best. You will automatically think of ideas and new ways to cook and present your food. You will become a master and you will get excited about it because it is the thing that expresses your love. Be excited about your life and your new start.

Analyze your life and decide upon those things that are empowering. Allow your mind to feel the achievement. You do not need your mind to prove to you that you can achieve this. You just need to see it and do it, **but do not sit on it**. Earlier I asked you, did you ever have an idea or dream about doing something and you never did anything about it. Then, sometime later you see where someone was doing what you never did, and you think or say, "Wow, I thought about doing that a long time ago." Or, you speak about doing something only the people you were speaking to could have heard it? Then sometime later, you see where someone (completely unrelated or elsewhere) is doing what you spoke of? Think about God's blessings to you. If you give your child something that you believe to be helpful to them in accomplishing something and they don't want to use it. What do you do? You take that thing away and give it to someone who needs it and can appreciate it. I believe God does the same with us. Don't be inattentive to yourself and your gifts from God. Become all that there is to become in your life.

Move: A Simple Understanding to Achieving

Chapter 5

Setting Your Goals, Visualizing Your Dreams, and

Making the Changes

God has already given you the gift of dreaming about what you should be doing. In your Passport Book (*at the end of this book*), this is the first thing you right on the first page. Write down what it is that you want to do. Think about what you want to achieve, no matter how large it is. If you have smaller goals to reach write them down and use them to reach the bigger goal, but make sure you are being specific. Visualize yourself achieving it. Write it down in big letters. This will be your focus, your love, your dream. To visualize yourself achieving your goal means that you can actually see yourself doing it. It does not matter how big the goal is, you must be able to visualize what you want.

Remember your focus. Most people will only do what makes them comfortable. These people are the ones who are only interested in their goals. Anybody can be interested in a goal, including you.

When there is a goal to be met there has to be a process set forth to accomplish it. Get committed to yourself and your goal. You must profess the goal. Say it out loud to yourself. Then write it down. In doing this it awakens the brain to get you moving. Look at it every day. Think about the specifics of accomplishing the goal and create a TO DO LIST. Start your list by writing in list form the things you already know that you have to do to reach this goal. Then, do some research to find out if there are other things you have to do to reach your goal. Sometimes knowing what needs to be done is half the road traveled to reaching your goal.

Example:

My Goal (Buy a Bigger House) TO DO List

> 1. *I need to work on clearing my credit*
>   a. *Order a credit report*
>   b. *Call creditor and find out about payment plans.*

2. *Decide what kind of payments I want I can afford.*
3. *Get a pre-approval from a lender.*
4. *Figure what my total cost would be to move.*
5. *What is my time frame?*

There will be much more to your TO DO List. Always add details when you think of them, and as you find them out. Remember that others do not have the same mission as you, so you cannot expect for everyone to fall in line with you. There will be times of difficulty, but you have a new mind now and difficulty is not a problem. It is a stepping stone. Difficulty is a learning opportunity for you. Take advantage of it, and step back for a second and look at it, evaluate it and keep your goal in sight.

Get ready for the process and do not allow fear to grab hold of you. It is natural to be unsure of what you do not know, but remember that you know where you are going and what you are about to do.

Just because you have never done it before does not mean that it is unknown. This is your planning stage. Take your To Do List and put your items in order of accomplishment. Whatever it is that you know already on your TO DO LIST is easier and needs to be completed first. If you need some type of education, then go find out where you can get that education the cheapest. If you need finances, figure out how you are either going to make the funds, or find out how you are going to get it (just don't steal it…ha ha ha).

If there is something you think is standing in your way, remember what I said about excuses and the reasons we claim to not do something. When you start to see these things pop up in your mind, you need to go right back to your goals and read them again. Make this a habit. Always read your goals. Train your mind to think about your goals all the time. Make it so that there is no room for anything negative to pop up. Be repetitive. Give your mind instructions on what to focus on. Take control and own your goals. Get back to loving yourself.

What are your habits? Do you talk to God daily? Create new habits for your new goals. You may be used to getting up in the morning after 9 am. Try getting up earlier; get your day going earlier. Give yourself more time in the day to work on your goals. Maybe you are used to coming home and laying everything down and watching television. Try something different. Try coming home, take a short nap, and then get up and read your goals and do some thinking about moving yourself forward.

You have to believe that you can and will do it. When you start believing that you can do it, your body starts to move in the direction that you are seeing yourself going in. You have already started the process of changing your mind, and now that your mind is changing, step up your belief system.

Believe that you will do it and that God is with you. Set yourself up to express your love and faith.

Use your Passport Book to take notes, paste images, remind yourself of ideas. These are the things that are and will be in your path to achieving your goals. I call it your Passport because this is your distinctive path to your goal. These are the things that will remind you of who you are, where you have been and where are you going. Even though there may be others who have accomplished what you want to do, you are an individual and your understanding of things may be different than others. Your path may be different than those in your circle of friends and family. In some cases you may have to change your circle of friends, love family members from a distance, change your environment, or even your job. Remember, your choices are yours. From this point on, where you are is because you chose to be there.

Don't forget to open your mind and spirit to your abilities. You were given a gift, so use your gift along the way to help you reach your goal. You will be surprised how your gift will grow and you become a master at what you do.

Most people fail to achieve because of this process. Making the necessary changes is the biggest part of achieving. It is a commonly known fact that changes are difficult, but knowing that you have to make a change and actually making the change can seem worlds apart. When it is time to change something, it means something has to be done away with (2 things cannot occupy the same space at once—Quantum Physics) and something different must replace it.

For example; if you have a task that takes 3 hours of your time in a day, but you feel like you do not have enough hours in the day to accomplish or achieve this task, do not make that the reason for you not doing anything. No excuses. You have to find more hours somehow in your day to accomplish this. If you are a late sleeper, you can replace your sleep and wake up a few hours earlier to work on your task. If you have activities in your day that really do not contribute to your achieving your goals, then you can change those activities and do something towards accomplishing your task.

Your current habits are what has gotten you this far, but if you are stuck at the level or place you are in, then your habits and belief system needs to change. You have to ask yourself what are your daily patterns or rituals? How do you start your day? Do you read your written goals? Creating new habits are the best way to gain control over your current situation. Your habits and your beliefs are what cause you to think in the way that you do. If you do not like the way things are turning out, then change the way you do things and change the way you think. Change your mind. Your brain controls all that you do--your behavior. Your behavior is a result of your experiences and what you have allowed yourself to think about your experiences. Regardless of what your experiences may have taught you, you cannot allow them to set up fear and control what your brain thinks out of fear. So what if you had a bad experience. You have things to accomplish, and a goal to reach. Give yourself affirmations and pray for strength to get you over the thing in your way. Talk to yourself and tell yourself to get up and move. Don't be in your own way. Breaking habits, especially the ones that are no good to you anymore is a key ingredient. This will release you from being committed to an old idea. It worked for you for a time, but now it's time to upgrade your thinking and your behavior.

A Message to Those of You Who Influence the Youth

As you work to become a better person, your influence on the youth will become stronger too. Young people admire those who show them that there is more to the world than what they are doing. They like to see the power that comes from doing the things that their parents talked about. Never think that you are not a role model. If there are any young people in your life, you can believe that they are watching you. They are trying to determine if you are worth their time to watch. Being honest with and loving yourself, as well as expressing honesty and love to others, allows them to see that they can live this way too.

You becoming greater expresses mastery of yourself and all that you have. Young people respect the show of mastery, especially the kind that commands them to be their best first. Just like the child always thinks about themselves first, you are relearning how to put your goals and life first. I am not saying to be selfish because selfishness does not make a good person. However, I am saying that you need to be mindful that you are being watched from the moment you begin to change. Now that you have stepped out on yourself and loving yourself, moving forward and becoming what you have dreamed to be; you are a better example of responsibility to the youth, a role model, as well as a teacher.

Teach them that they too can be what they want to be and dream about. Teach them that it is a good time in their life to recognize that should do everything they can to be who they are supposed to be. Ask them about being interested or committed in themselves. Ask them if they want to be achievers and not just dreamers. Staying in school and being excellent students is the most important thing they can do for themselves at this age. It is not an option to quit or say that they cannot do something. The impossible is the easiest to reach while they are still living in a time of grace in their young lives.

Our young people need to know that it is the smart thing to do when they make conscious decisions about their future. Now is the time for them to look within and get to know who they are, feel who they are, see who they are, and experience their true selves. No one can stop them from being who God intended for them to be.

Move: A Simple Understanding to Achieving

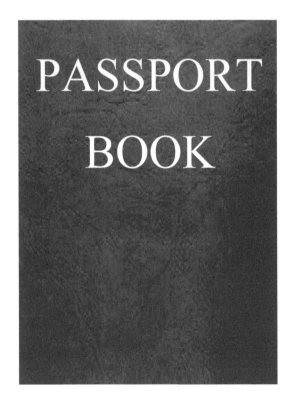

What Do I See Yourself Doing?
What Do I Want To Do?
(Write down these things, paste pictures, use symbols)

What Are My Gifts?

To Do List

What are the other things I found that I need to do that I did not know about?

What Are My Habits?

Notes/Images/Affirmations